Sexual Immorality

■ ■ ■

Addiction of Loss

By Prince Handley

University of Excellence Press

Copyright © 2016 by Prince Handley
All Rights Reserved.

UNIVERSITY OF EXCELLENCE PRESS
Los Angeles ▪ London ▪ Tel Aviv

ISBN-13: 978-0692671962
ISBN-10: 069267196X

First Edition

The only Sexual Attitudes book you need!

TABLE OF CONTENTS

FOREWORD

Recently I received a phone call from a Christian brother who confessed to me that he had being having sex with a woman—**a friend of their family**—and asking me to pray for him. His wife was getting ready to leave.

This book is NOT only about marital infidelity ... it is about sexual immorality for single people as well.

How would you like to **protect yourself from sexual impropriety PLUS**—at the same time—**learn HOW to be used in SPECIAL works for the LORD?**

You will in this book ... AND ... you will learn about the **secret "behind–the–scenes" stratagem** to hurt you, to bring you down, to destroy you and to bring you into dishonor.

You will learn WHY NOT and HOW NOT to succumb to temptation—how to be strong and victorious.

In addition, if you have fallen prey to attacks of sexual misconduct, **you will learn how to turn the situation around with a NEW start and recover loss**—LOSS that you surrendered by CHOICE through temptation. But, more importantly, **you will learn the JOY of forgiveness and fellowship with God: your best friend**.

You will learn God's plan of protection—*to keep you*—and, if necessary, restoration, redemption and recovery.

YOU can be God's friend!

Sexual Immorality

■ ■ ■

Addiction of Loss

FOUR THINGS TO KNOW
ABOUT SEXUAL IMMORALITY
(1 Corinthians 6:12-20)

- It will hurt you and rule over you.

- It is not good for your body.

- It should make us run away.

- It dishonors God.

6

LET'S EXAMINE THESE FOUR

⬤ **It will hurt you and rule over you.**

"All things are lawful for me, but all things are <u>not helpful</u>. All things are lawful for me, but I will not be brought <u>under the power</u> of any." (Verse 12)

⬤ **It is not good for your body.**

"Now the body is not for sexual immorality but for the Lord, and the Lord for the body. And God both raised up the Lord and will also raise us up by His power.

*Do you not know that your bodies are members of Christ? Shall I then take the members of Christ and make them members of a prostitute or whore? Certainly not! Or, do you not know that **he** who is joined to a* *woman is one body with her? For "the two," God says, "shall become one flesh."* [Torah: Genesis 2:24] *"But he who is joined to the Lord is one spirit with Him." (Verses 13-17)*

This is why we need to commit to marriage before we have sexual relations.

It should make us run away.

"Run away from sexual immorality. Every sin that a man does is outside the body, but he who commits sexual immorality sins against his own body." (Verse 18)

It dishonors God.

"Or do you not know that your body is the temple of the Holy Spirit who is in you, whom you have from God, and you are not your own? For you were bought with a price; therefore glorify God in your body and in your spirit, which are God's." (Verse 19-20)

8

ALL THINGS START WITH A THOUGHT

What you think or what you image—all start in the mind: the soulish realm. You are a tripartite being. Just as there is a Divine Trinity: God, the Father; God, the Son; and God, the Holy Spirit … so are **you a threefold personality: spirit, soul and body**.

Your human spirit interfaces between God and your soul ("nephesh" in Hebrew). Your soul comprises intellect, emotion and will. **What you think or see in your mind (image or imagination) is the progenitor of what you will do in your body**. That's WHY you must learn to control your thoughts and images.

Learn to build a wall. Delete the BAD thoughts and images before they can spread, grow and develop into actions like cancer. Learn to take your thoughts and images CAPTIVE and CAST THEM DOWN. In 2 Corinthians 10:3-5 we read:

*"For though we walk in the flesh, **we do not war***

9

according to the flesh. For the weapons of our warfare are not fleshly but mighty through God for pulling down strongholds, casting down arguments and every high thing that exalts itself against the knowledge of God, bringing into captivity every thought to the obedience of Christ."

I used to live on my yacht and because of that spent a lot of time on the beach. At sunset I used to visualize the greatness of God from the expanse of ocean from the Pacific Coast westward. It helped me to think creatively. It reminds me of a story about a man who was on the beach and prayed to God, asking for God to build a bridge from California to Hawaii. God answered the man, *"I can do that easily, but wouldn't you rather have something of more benefit to you?"* The man thought, and answered, *"Yes, God, can you help me to understand women?"* The Lord replied, *"Do you want that bridge to be four lanes or six lanes?"*

You can talk to God. He understands your situation. Ask Him for help. **When you are tempted with sexual immorality, learn to say to the LORD, *"Jesus, do you***

want to do this with me?" And, if you can't ask that question—*or feel uncomfortable asking it*—then you know NOT to perform the action.

Just because it feels good does NOT make it good. In Genesis 3:6 we read that Eve thought the fruit was:

Good for food	Appetite	Lust of the flesh
Pleasant to the eyes	Appeal	Lust of the eyes
Desired to make one wise	Applause	Pride of life

But in 1 John 2:16 we read that, *"For all that is in the world—the lust of the flesh, the lust of the eyes, and the pride of life—is not of the Father but is of the world."* And in verse 17, *"And the world is passing away, and the lust of it; but he who does the will of God abides forever."*

Here is a SECRET to help you. And … I think it is really what holiness is about. When you start your day, pray and **ask God to give you the desire to please Him MORE than you want to lust, commit fornication or view pornography**.

In the USA, 77% of men and 25% of women either do watch or have watched pornography ... with a high percentage of those being people involved in the work of the LORD.

If you have been—or are—operating in an alternative life style such as gay, lesbian, transgender, bisexual or queer, **KNOW that God can deliver you**. He will forgive you, cleanse you and give you a NEW start. Do NOT let people, institutions, philosophies or friends deceive you and keep you out of God's BEST for YOU—and out of Heaven.

In the Torah, Genesis 2:24, we read: *"Therefore a man shall leave his father and mother and be joined to his wife, and they shall become one flesh."* The institution of the family unit—**marriage based upon a man and his wife**—was for procreation of the race: to produce children. This is why our bodies are made such: with a man's penis and a woman's vagina. And this is the only combination that produces a natural God ordained fertilized egg in the woman.

Reading the context of **Genesis Chapter 19** we can easily see **God's view of—and the judgment on— homosexuality**. Also, in Romans 1:24-28 of the New Testament, we read:

> *"Therefore **God also gave them up to uncleanness, in the lusts of their hearts, to dishonor their bodies among themselves**, who exchanged the truth of God for the lie, and worshiped and served the creature rather than the Creator, who is blessed forever. Amen.*

> *For this reason **God gave them up to vile passions. For even their women exchanged the natural use for what is against nature. Likewise, also the men, leaving the natural use of the woman, burned in their lust for one another, men with men committing what is***

shameful, and receiving in themselves the penalty of their error which was due. And even as they did not like to retain God in their knowledge, God gave them over to a debased mind, to do those things which are not fitting."

I have a good friend who is in Heaven with the LORD now who founded and directed for years a powerful ministry in a large metroplex. He was a wonderful husband and father with a beautiful wife and children, all who still love and serve God. One time after we preached together he shared with me his testimony. **He had been a male prostitute**—a homosexual who hired himself out—**and realized he was lost and on his way to Hell**. He gave his life to Christ and was wonderfully transformed. He eventually married the girl who had witnessed to him which resulted in his salvation. And they lived a wonderful family life.

I say this to share with you that you're never too far gone. **Jesus loves you so much ... He gave His life for you on the cross. His body and brain took your punishment ... His BLOOD paid for your sins.** Ask the Lord Jesus to deliver you. And if you want other help, counsel or encouragement, there are many places that will help you. And, you can always contact me at the Email listed above. I will be happy to pray for you.

Remember—thoughts, images, flirting—all put you one step closer to the actions. Learn to stop them in their tracks. If you have a problem at the office with flirting or temptation, put a picture of your family—*or a photo of the Bible or an Angel*—on your phone or on your desk. Build a wall between you and the problem to keep the "fiery darts" of temptation deflected. Get involved in praying in the Spirit, in tongues, or in God's Work. **Faith quenches the fiery darts of the wicked one**. *"Above all, taking the shield of faith with which you will be able to **quench all the fiery darts** of the wicked one."* (Ephesians 6:16)

Think these … say these >> I want to please God – I want to be God's friend – I want to live holy!

I trust teaching helps you, my friend. **Heaven is REAL … and it is forever**. Don't miss it.

And ... remember this BONUS: If you want to be used in SPECIAL works for the LORD, live a separated life. So now we will study: **The Power of a Separated Life**.

THE POWER OF A SEPARATED LIFE

After I became a follower of Messiah Yeshua I committed quality time to memorizing scripture. One of the key Bible portions I memorized was as follows:

"Do not be unequally yoked together with unbelievers: for what fellowship has righteousness with unrighteousness? And, what communion has light with darkness?

Wherefore come out from among them, and you be separate, says the Lord, and touch not the unclean thing; and I will receive you.

And I will be a Father unto you, and you shall be my sons and daughters, says the Lord Almighty." [Brit Chadashah: 2 Corinthians 6:14, 17-18]

I didn't have to leave my friends when I became a believer; they left me! When my lifestyle became different and my interests were focused in Godly avenues, there was no common ground. However, I still talked to my friends about the Lord, and prayed for them, and loved them with Messiah's compassion. Thankfully, many of them are now followers of Yeshua who serve the Lord, including my immediate birth family, uncles, aunts, cousins ... and now all of my children and grandchildren.

What a beautiful promise! God will be a Father to us: **He will protect us, provide for us, and be personal in His relationship to us**. Do you want to have a REALLY CLOSE walk with the Lord? **Then learn and practice the beauty of a separated life**.

In this teaching we will study the PURPOSE, the PRIVILEGE, the PROTECTION, and the PRODUCTIVITY of a separated life.

THE PURPOSE OF A SEPARATED LIFE

Why live a separated life?

"As obedient children, not fashioning yourselves according to the former lusts in your ignorance: But as He which has called you is holy, so you be holy in all manner of behavior; because it is written, 'You be holy, for I am holy'." [Leviticus 11:45; 1 Peter 1:15-16]

THE PRIVILEGE OF SEPARATION

Why is it a privilege to live a separated life?

"For as much as you know that you were not redeemed with corruptible things, like silver and gold, from your vain manner of living which you received by tradition from your fathers; but you were redeemed with the precious blood of Messiah, as of a lamb without blemish and without spot: who truly was foreordained BEFORE the foundation of the world, but was manifest in these last times for YOU." [1 Peter 1:18-20]

"According as He has CHOSEN us in Him BEFORE the foundation of the world, that we should be holy and without blame before Him in love." [Ephesians 1:4]

THE PROTECTION OF SEPARATION

Living a separated life of holiness unto the Lord provides extra angelic protection for the believer.

"The angel of the Lord encamps around those that fear Him and delivers them." [Psalm 34:7]

"Because you have made the Lord, which is my refuge, even the Most High, your habitation; there shall no evil befall you, neither shall any plague come near your dwelling. For He shall give his angels charge over you, to keep you in all your ways." [Psalm 91:9-11 – read the whole Psalm]

"And he answered, fear not: for they that be with us are more than they that be with them. And Elisha prayed, and said, Lord, I pray thee, open his eyes, that he may

see. And the Lord opened the eyes of the young man; and he saw: and, behold, the mountain was full of horses and chariots of fire round about Elisha." [2 Kings 6:16-17]

Other examples: Daniel in the den of lions and the three Hebrew teenagers in the furnace of fire. These were Hebrews, who as teenagers had separated themselves unto God.

THE PRODUCTIVITY OF SEPARATION

Why is it productive to live a separated life?

"Let everyone that names the name of Christ depart from iniquity. But in a great house there are not only vessels of gold and of silver, but also of wood and earth; and some to honor, and some to dishonor.

If a person therefore cleanses himself from these [the works of dishonor and iniquity], he shall be a vessel unto honor, set apart, worthy, competent and profitable for the master's use, prepared unto every good work." [2 Timothy 2:19-21]

The greatest blessing you can have on earth is to walk with God!

Enoch walked with God, and he was not found anymore here on earth because God took him. [Genesis 5:24]

Elijah walked with God, and when it was time for him to go to Heaven, he was taken up by angels in a chariot surrounded by fire. [2 Kings 2:11]

You say, *"But Apostle Handley, these were SPECIAL people."* Yes, and **so are YOU . . . if you WANT to be**. They were special people because they wanted to be special people.

The question is: *"Do you WANT to be SPECIAL?"*

The Holy Bible shows us that Elijah was just like you and me. He had the same emotions, the same temptations, and the same faculties. *"Elijah was a man subject to like*

21

passions as we are, and he prayed earnestly that it might not rain: and it rained not on the earth by the space of three years and six months. And he prayed again, and the heaven gave rain, and the earth brought forth her fruit." [James 5:17-18]

As we approach the last days of Planet Earth and the return of Israel's Messiah we should all the more want to live a separated life. The Apostle Peter told us ahead of time:

"But the day of the Lord will come as a thief in the night; in the which the heavens shall pass away with a great noise, and the elements shall melt with fervent heat, the earth also and the works that are therein shall be burned up. Seeing then that all these things shall be dissolved, what manner of people should you be in all holy manner of living and godliness . . ." [2 Peter 3:10-11]

The Apostle Paul assigned Titus, a young preacher, the responsibility of pastoring and appointing elders in Crete and explained to him that it was **profitable for believers to maintain good works**. *"This is a faithful saying, and these things I will that you affirm constantly, that those*

22

people who have believed in God might be careful to maintain good works. These things are good and profitable unto men." [Titus 3:8]

Paul also taught Timothy, who he placed in charge of the church at Ephesus, that there is great gain in living for God. *"But godliness with contentment is great gain."* [1 Timothy 6:6]

If we are going to live a separated life so that we will be prepared to be used by the Master, then we have to be like a soldier. *"You therefore must endure hardship as a good soldier of Yeshua HaMashiach (Jesus the Messiah). No one engaged in warfare entangles himself with the affairs of this life, so that he may please him who enlisted him as a soldier."* [2 Timothy 2:3-4]

Holiness is the principle that separates the believer from the world. Holiness is a quality of personal conduct that consecrates us to God's service. The Apostle Paul urged the believers in his day . . . and urges us today through the scripture . . . to walk in holiness and thereby please God.

"For this is the will of God, your sanctification: that you should abstain from sexual immorality; that each of you should know how to possess his own vessel in sanctification and honor." [1 Thessalonians 4:3-4]

Notice, in the verse above, that YOU are to POSSESS your vessel: you are the owner . . . you are in control. Don't say *"The devil made me do it!"* Don't say, *"I couldn't resist!"* **Have you been struggling with a certain temptation? Then get on your knees and CRY OUT to God. Ask Him to deliver you and sanctify you**. The Bible says, *"Call upon me in the day of trouble: I will deliver you, and you shall glorify me."* [Psalm 50:15]

God is not dangling temptation in front of you to tempt you. *"Let no man say when he is tempted, I am tempted of God: for God cannot be tempted with evil, neither does he tempt anyone."* [James 1:13]

God has made a WAY for you to exit temptation, but you have to WANT to exit! *"There has NO temptation taken you but such as is common to man: but God is faithful,* who will not allow you to be tempted above that which you are able; but will with the temptation also make a way to escape, that you may be able to bear it." [1 Corinthians 10:13]

In the original Greek of which this passage was written it is actually saying that God will do the same as **cut a path through a rock for you to make a way for you to escape . . . IF you WANT to escape!** Cry out to Him and He will deliver you! God loves you and wants to help you. He also wants to use you to help others!

God may allow you to be tested from time to time, but **only to see if you are worthy of Him investing His future talents and gifts in you so that you can be used for GREAT WORKS**. What if after you have been used greatly, you mess up and ruin your testimony? Or, what if you make God or His people look bad?

Set apart a time for prayer and fasting to consecrate yourself to His service. Pray for a consecrated life: a life set apart in holiness and separation so you can be a vessel unto honor . . . worthy, competent, and profitable for the Master's use . . . prepared unto every good work.

The more you are in the arena and productive for God, the more you will be shot at! And there will be different times you will need to draw on God's strength through prayer and fasting. But always remember: **Your best defense is a good offense. Keep reaching people for Messiah . . . keep under the anointing!**

CONCLUSION

In this section we have studied the PURPOSE, the PRIVILEGE, the PROTECTION, and the PRODUCTIVITY of a separated life.

Why live holy?

● I want to be like my Father in Heaven.

● I am thankful for what Messiah Jesus has done for me.

- I want to be protected.
- I want to be used in special ways.

In this book we have learned:

- Four things to know about sexual immorality.
- All things start with a thought.
- Because it feels good does not make it good.
- How sexual immorality produces loss.
- How God can protect you.
- God delivers, heals and makes you strong.
- The purpose of a separated life.

Go with God, my friend, and enjoy a powerful, protected and productive life.

BE GOD'S FRIEND!

✝

OTHER BOOKS BY PRINCE HANDLEY

- Map of the End Times
- How to Do Great Works
- Flow Chart of Revelation
- Action Keys for Success
- Health and Healing Complete Guide to Wholeness
- Prophetic Calendar for Israel & the Nations: Thru 2023
- Healing Deliverance
- How to Receive God's Power with Gifts of the Spirit
- Healing for Mental and Physical Abuse
- Victory Over Opposition and Resistance
- Healing of Emotional Wounds
- How to Be Healed and Live in Divine Health
- Healing from Fear, Shame and Anger
- How to Receive Healing and Bring Healing to Others
- New Global Strategy: Enabling Missions
- The Art of Christian Warfare
- Success Cycles and Secrets
- New Testament Bible Studies (A Study Manual)
- Babylon the Bitch – Enemy of Israel
- Resurrection Multiplication – Miracle Production
- Faith and Quantum Physics – Your Future
- Conflict Healing – Relational Health
- Decision Making 101 – Know for Sure
- Total Person Toolbox
- Prophecy, Transition & Miracles
- Enhanced Humans – Mystery Matrix
- Israel and Middle East – Past Present Future
- Anarchy and revolution: A Prophecy
- Real Miracles for Normal People

AVAILABLE AT AMAZON AND OTHER BOOK STORES

In addition, check out the 99 cent FAST READ
Spiritual Growth Mini-Books by Prince Handley

SPIRITUAL GROWTH SERIES

UNIVERSITY OF EXCELLENCE PRESS
Los Angeles ■ London ■ Tel Aviv

BONUS

To help you, and to help you teach others, we have prepared FREE **Rabbinical Studies** at this site:

uofe.org/RABBINICAL_STUDIES.html

The above are commentaries from **ancient** Jewish Rabbis that identify the Mashiach of Israel.

Also, to help you, and to help you teach others, you will find Bible Studies in English, Spanish and French.

■ English FREE Bible Studies
uofe.org/english_bible_studies.html

■ Spanish FREE Bible Studies
uofe.org/spanish_bible_studies.html

■ French FREE Bible Studies
uofe.org/french_bible_studies.html

LIVE A LIFE OF EXCELLENCE

Email for seminars to:
princehandley@gmail.com

UNIVERSITY OF EXCELLENCE PRESS
Los Angeles ■ London ■ Tel Aviv

NOTE

We listen to our readers. Tell us what **new** subject matter you would like to see published. Email your ideas to: universityofexcellence@gmail.com